Be a Queen

Serving Cvnt

Cause a Scene

SERVING CVNT

Copyright © Octopus Publishing Group Limited, 2025

All rights reserved.

Text by Marianne Thompson

No part of this book may be reproduced by any means, nor transmitted, nor translated into a machine language, without the written permission of the publishers.

Condition of Sale
This book is sold subject to the condition that it shall not, by way of trade or otherwise, be lent, resold, hired out or otherwise circulated in any form of binding or cover other than that in which it is published and without a similar condition including this condition being imposed on the subsequent purchaser.

An Hachette UK Company
www.hachette.co.uk

Summersdale Publishers
Part of Octopus Publishing Group Limited
Carmelite House
50 Victoria Embankment
LONDON
EC4Y 0DZ
UK

www.summersdale.com

This FSC® label means that materials and other controlled sources used for the product have been responsibly sourced

The authorized representative in the EEA is Hachette Ireland, 8 Castlecourt Centre, Dublin 15, D15 XTP3, Ireland (email: info@hbgi.ie)

Printed and bound in Poland

ISBN: 978-1-83799-906-4
eISBN: 978-1-83799-907-1

Substantial discounts on bulk quantities of Summersdale books are available to corporations, professional associations and other organizations. For details contact general enquiries: telephone: +44 (0) 1243 771107 or email: enquiries@summersdale.com.

To _____

From _____

Disclaimer

Every effort has been made to ensure that the information in this book is hot AF. The publisher cannot be held accountable for the extreme levels of devastating cvntiness that may result from following any of the advice mentioned herein.

Hey, gurrrl!

So, you wanna serve cvnt? Babe, we got you. Serving cvnt is the boldest, fiercest way to slay. Cvnt is a *mood* – it's all about owning your power, expressing yourself fully and living your life on your own terms. You may be asking, "When can I serve cvnt?" or "Where can I serve cvnt?" and the answer is… "Yes."

> If it's not bold, if it's not ruffling feathers, what's the point?

— CHAPPELL ROAN

A strong spirit transcends rules.

PRINCE

BE A QUEEN, CAUSE A SCENE

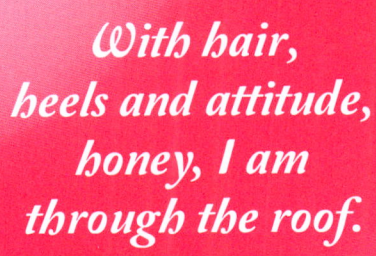

People will always talk, so let's give them something to talk about.

LADY GAGA

Better to live one year as a tiger than a hundred as a sheep.

MADONNA

Attitude is everything

Nothing is more unapologetically cvnty than killer confidence. It's the foundation on which cvntiness is built. Darling, you're not here to check the vibes – you *are* the vibes. Attitude is *essential* to serving cvnt, so don't be afraid to put yourself out there and bring your energy to the room.

BE THE WHOLE MEAL, NOT JUST THE SNACK

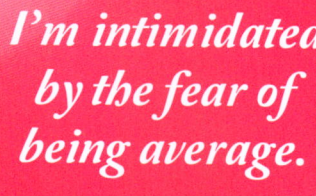

> It's nobody's responsibility to cover themselves or restrict or restrain themselves for somebody else's, like, weak willpower. It's not our job.

BILLIE EILISH

I find only freedom in the realms of eccentricity.

DAVID BOWIE

It's not your job to like me, it's mine.

BYRON KATIE

I'm a master-piece

Be authentic

Be fierce, be free and be fearlessly *you*. You don't exist to filter yourself for the sake of others – you should never censor your sass. Only you can be *you* and if someone doesn't like it, that's their problem. The less you care about how other people view you, the cvntier your aura will be; give zero fucks and your inner circle will respect your realness.

I want things to look a certain way. Not because it makes me look gay, or it makes me look straight, or it makes me look bisexual, but because I think it looks cool.

HARRY STYLES

Who you are is beautiful and amazing.

LAVERNE COX

I think we're always growing and shifting and moving and being reborn in some way... the closer you feel to yourself, there's nothing but joy there.

SAM SMITH

RIOT, don't diet

I want to be remembered as the girl who stood up.

MALALA YOUSAFZAI

Love your body

Got deadly curves, legs for days or a lethal face card? **Show. It. Off.** Remember, cvnty isn't a size or shape – it's a state of being. Every inch of your being is *divine*, so if you think you have flaws, honey, they're *flawsome*. You're a goddess, so let everyone bask in your glow… and don't let those salty bitches try to bring you down.

All the marks on the world mean nothing compared to the marks you're about to make.

AMBER TAMBLYN

Sometimes you gotta be a beauty and a beast.

NICKI MINAJ

> I'm done compromising; even more so, I'm done with being compromised.
>
> — MILA KUNIS

I was not bern to be subtle

I'm on the path to being someone I'm equally terrified by and obsessed with. My true self.

TROYE SIVAN

There's no better makeup than self-confidence.

SHAKIRA

Dress to impress

You're not here to blend in – you're here to be discussed. Your wardrobe is essential to making every moment *the* moment. You can never be overdressed (or *underdressed*), so be bold, be brave and be badass with your fashion choices. Of course, it isn't always what you wear, hon, it's how you wear it; cvnt is a mindset, not just a look, so clothes that make you *feel* confident *are* cvnty.

I think something happens when you get to a certain point in your life where you just kind of stop caring and you just start living.

SABRINA CARPENTER

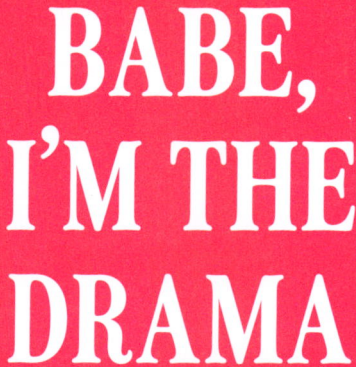

I finally got my answer to that question: Who do you think you are? I am whoever I say I am.

AMERICA FERRERA

You have to stand for what you believe in and sometimes you have to stand alone.

QUEEN LATIFAH

A girl doesn't need anyone who doesn't need her.

MARILYN MONROE

Accessorize

Sunglasses, heels or a feather boa can all serve cvnt, but sometimes you just need a little, or *a lot*, more from your added extras. For truly *unhinged* levels of cvntiness, you could accessorize with oversized or non-typical accessories and watch eyes widen as you enter the room. Be shocking, babe; it's *sooo* much fun!

I AM THAT BITCH

My coach said I ran like a girl. I said if he ran a little faster he could too.

MIA HAMM

> **If you're operating from a genuine place, then you can't really regret anything.**
>
> — KRISTEN STEWART

I always knew I was a star. And now, the rest of the world seems to agree with me.

FREDDIE MERCURY

50% brat, 50% yap

Squad goals

Being a strong, independent girlboss doesn't mean being alone; even the most confident of baddies needs her bitches. If you're feeling low, call on your girls to fix the vibes, spill the tea and *yap, yap, yap.* Your squad also needs you as much as you need them, and a true queen should be ready to support her sisterhood *no matter what.*

*Be brave,
be bold,
be free.*

ANGELINA JOLIE

I'm used to people being irritated by me. I'm like, girl, whatever. Be irritated. I'm gonna live my dream.

BOB THE DRAG QUEEN

Be iconic

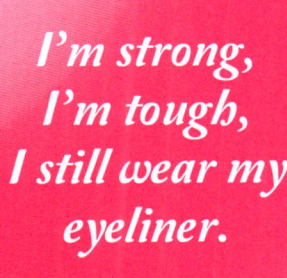

I'm strong, I'm tough, I still wear my eyeliner.

LISA LESLIE

> **Being different is a talent. You illuminate what makes you special in the sea of sameness around you.**
>
> LADY GAGA

I just love bossy women… It means somebody's passionate and engaged and ambitious and doesn't mind leading.

AMY POEHLER

Fit check

When you're looking snatched, it's time for a fit check to show off that new look. You know it's cvnty, but perhaps you are simply wondering, "Is it cvnty *enough*?" You gotta snap that selfie and send it straight to the group chat – you're hot, and your girls are going to confirm that your fit is *fire*.

I ate and left no crumbs

Girls got balls. They're just a little higher up.

JOAN JETT

> *I have moments where I am worried, and I'm like, "Maybe I should dial it back because that's a little too honest," but I don't give a fuck because I know that in the end, it's going to pay off more for me to be real.*
>
> — DOECHII

The best protection any woman can have is courage.

ELIZABETH CADY STANTON

Take a chance and don't ever look back. Never have regrets, just lessons learned.

KIM KARDASHIAN

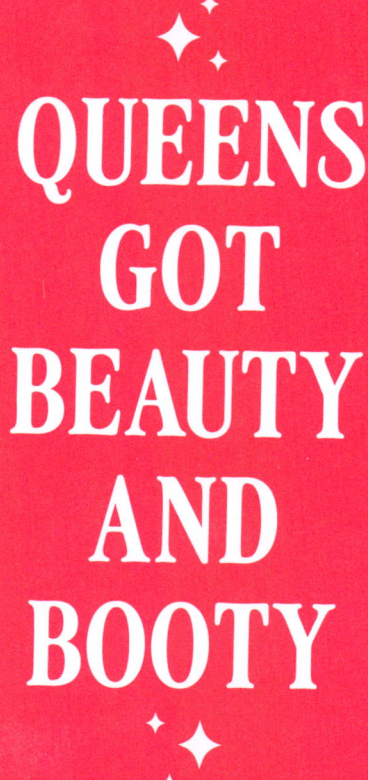

Body language

With the tilt of your head or the arch of your *perfect* brow, you can say *everything* without saying *anything*. Sip a drink while you knowingly gaze across the room or blow a flirty kiss over your shoulder as you part company; you can be saucy, sexy *and* sophisticated without uttering a single word.

I'm not terribly interested in beauty. What touches me is someone who understands herself.

VIVIENNE WESTWOOD

If you don't like the road you're walking, start paving another one.

DOLLY PARTON

Girl power is almost more powerful and more special than anything we are competing for.

SELENA GOMEZ

I'VE GOT SASS AND ASS

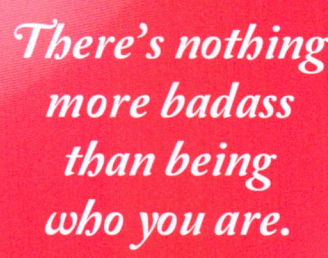

Maybe you aren't meant to fit in. Maybe you're meant to stand out.

TAYLOR SWIFT

Walk the walk

The world is your catwalk, so channel your inner supermodel and strut like you own the room – because *you do*. Heels are optional, but sass is not, and lethal posture is the core of a walk that slays hard *and* turns heads. Start by lowering your chin slightly, then drop your shoulders and relax your arms. As you walk, put one foot slightly in front of the other and let that cake sway! Leave your spectators whispering, "She *ate* and left *no* crumbs."

Bite me

A dame that knows the ropes isn't likely to get tied up.

MAE WEST

My motto is: I'm alive. So that means I can do anything.

VENUS WILLIAMS

Unless they gonna pay your bills, pay them bitches no mind.

RuPAUL

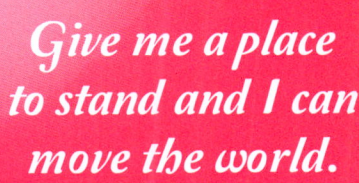

Babes support babes

Accept nothing but the fact that you're equal.

NEKO CASE

Strike a pose

"*She* has arrived", and by "she" they mean "you". It's time to make a statement and serve up your signature stance with a side of sass. When you need to strike a pose, imagination is the limit, girl! A hand on the hip is always classic... but can you make it *more* cvnty? Everyone is watching, so be scandalous with your angles and exhibit a work of art.

Other women who are killing it should motivate you, thrill you, challenge you and inspire you.

TAYLOR SWIFT

You're born to be who you are.

SABRINA CARPENTER

I'm doing hot girl shit

Do what you are afraid to do.

MILEY CYRUS

Any time you're putting barriers up in your own life, you're just limiting yourself.

HARRY STYLES

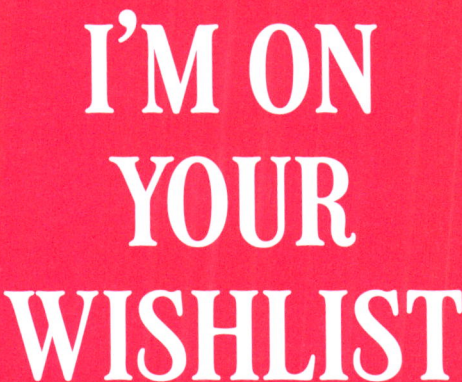

Make an entrance… and an exit

Everyone should know when you've entered the room, but they should also know when you've left it. You want your absence to be as big as your presence, which sometimes means that the best way to slay is simply to walk away. You want everyone to wonder what it is that *you* know, and *they* don't. Your exit is your mic drop moment, so turn on that heel and **Strut. Your. Stuff**.

We need to laugh at the haters and sympathize with them. They can scream as loud as they want. We can't hear them because we are getting shit done.

AMY SCHUMER

*I've always
played it my way.*

CHARLI XCX

> I'm gonna make what I want to make, and other people are gonna like what they're gonna like.
>
> — BILLIE EILISH

THANKS, BUT I DIDN'T ASK YOU

I like to be surrounded by splendid things.

FREDDIE MERCURY

If your dreams do not scare you, they are not big enough.

ELLEN JOHNSON SIRLEAF

Throw shade

Need to throw shade? Babe, it's all in the side-eye. The key to serving ice is to speak with the eyes, but not with the rest of the face. Try glancing, narrowing or rolling your eyes while keeping your lower face as neutral as possible. With a single, devastating glance, you can let your enemies know you're unimpressed... with zero effort.

I never underestimated myself. And I never saw anything wrong with ambition.

ANGELA MERKEL

Eat. Me. Up.

If you put that effort in, you'll get what you want.

KIM KARDASHIAN

You have what it takes to be a victorious, independent, fearless woman.

TYRA BANKS

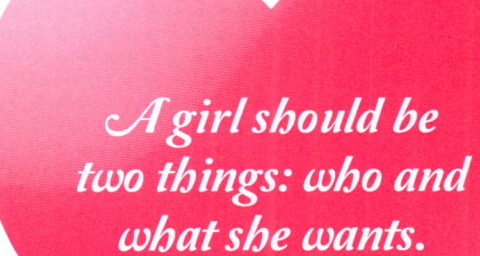

A girl should be two things: who and what she wants.

COCO CHANEL

Feeling cvnty

Slay it with words

Confidence is the essence of cvnty conversation; it's not always about what you say, it's *how* you say it. A whisper can be gentle, but it can also be deadly, babe. Of course, it's also all about what you *don't* say; well-timed pauses can leave them hanging on... to... your... every... word.

If you know you're great at what you do, don't ever be ashamed to ask for the top dollar in your field.

NICKI MINAJ

I'd rather regret the things I've done than regret the things I haven't done.

LUCILLE BALL

I'm tough, I'm ambitious, and I know exactly what I want.

MADONNA

I stand by every mistake I've ever made, so judge away.

KRISTEN STEWART

You are valued, you are a goddess and don't forget that.

JENNIFER LOPEZ

Know your worth, then add tax

Give nothing

Silence can speak a thousand words, but your silence is going to shout MYSTERY. Arrive, give them absolutely nothing and leave them wondering, "Who *is* she?"

> I'm not the next Usain Bolt or Michael Phelps. I'm the first Simone Biles.
>
> — SIMONE BILES

A wise girl knows her limits but a smart girl knows she has none.

MARILYN MONROE

Be so good they can't ignore you.

STEVE MARTIN

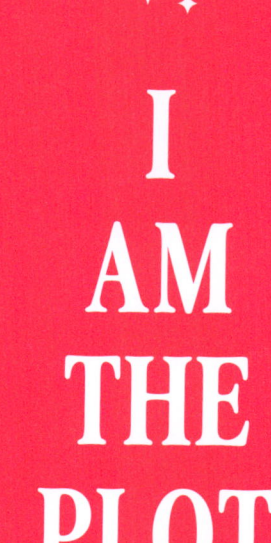

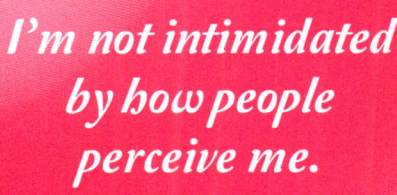

If you help someone else succeed, you too shall succeed. I rise when others rise.

GINA RODRIGUEZ

Be the drama

So, you're a hot mess right now? Who cares? You're the main character in your life, so bring that energy to the table. Always. Haters gonna hate, so you may as well give them something to yap about. Girl, let chaos be your company and dare them to speculate, "What *will* she do next?"

> Just try new things. Don't be afraid. Step out of your comfort zones and soar.
>
> MICHELLE OBAMA

MY VIBES ARE SACRED

I've been through it all, baby. I'm mother courage.

ELIZABETH TAYLOR

Nothing can dim the light which shines from within.

MAYA ANGELOU

When you become the image of your own imagination, it's the most powerful thing you could ever do.

RuPAUL

I would rather die of passion than of boredom.

ÉMILE ZOLA

Slay all day

Be extra, be iconic

A true diva keeps everyone guessing what her next move will be, so be spontaneous and unpredictable whenever you're feeling it. You're the plot *and* the twist, baby! Show up fashionably late to an event, wear something totally *outrageous*, or dance when no one else wants to (*especially* when no one else wants to).

> Be a girl
> with a mind,
> a bitch with an
> attitude, and a
> lady with class.

RIHANNA

Don't be afraid to speak up for yourself. Keep fighting for your dreams!

GABBY DOUGLAS

*If you rest,
you rust.*

HELEN HAYES

Future MILF

You need to find the power within to make things happen for yourself. When you realize this, you are unstoppable.

CHRISTINA AGUILERA

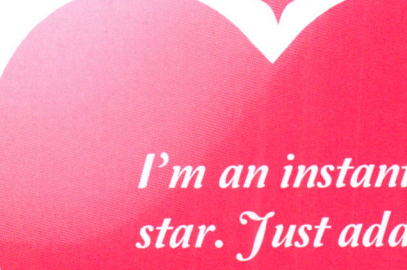

Don't ask permission

Who tells you what to do? No one. You're a babe with the power and you do what you want, when you want. You're not bossy; you're *the* boss. Darling, only *you* can live your life and that means you should never put yourself in second place or let others shape your narrative. If you have to ask anything, it should only ever be, "Did I serve *enough* cvnt today?"

> You can,
> you should, and if
> you're brave enough
> to start, you will.

STEPHEN KING

I figure, if a girl wants to be a legend, she should just go ahead and be one.

CALAMITY JANE

I'm a mood

I've never been interested in being invisible and erased.

LAVERNE COX

I am the most important character in this movie. This is my motherfucking movie.

DOECHII

*If you feel
like you look good,
you look good.*

BILLIE EILISH

Set the trends

You weren't born to follow trends, hon, you were born to set them. You have the power to bestow cvntiness upon that which you deem worthy, but you should also use this power wisely; if everything is cvnty then *nothing* is cvnty. Scarcity creates demand (and your opinion should always be *in demand*), so be exclusive and be selective with your choices.

A strong woman looks a challenge dead in the eye and gives it a wink.

GINA CAREY

I've erased the word "fear" from my vocabulary, and I think when you erase fear, you can't fail.

ALICIA KEYS

TOO GLAM TO GIVE A DAMN

I want people to walk around delusional about how great they can be.

LADY GAGA

I never understood the idea that you're supposed to mellow as you get older. Slowing down isn't something I relate to at all. The goal is to continue in good and bad, all of it.

DIANE KEATON

Have passions

Maybe you love embroidery? Very cvnty. Or you can lip-sync a whole album? Definitely cvnty. Or perhaps you can play Beethoven's fifth symphony? *Sooo* cvnty. It doesn't matter where your talents lie – passion is powerful. You're a talent *with* talents and you never know when you're going to need to put on a show! Hone those hobbies and you'll be the most interesting person in the room.

OUT HERE MAKING SHIT HAPPEN

If you can believe
in something great,
then you can achieve
something great.

KATY PERRY

I believe ambition is not a dirty word. It's just believing in yourself and your abilities.

REESE WITHERSPOON

*I am not
a has-been.
I am a will be.*

LAUREN BACALL

Always be a first-rate version of yourself, instead of a second-rate version of somebody else.

JUDY GARLAND

Karma is *my* bitch

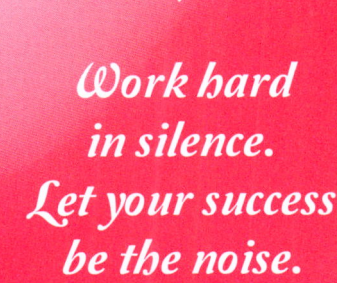

I think that not being perfect has given me the freedom to keep getting better.

GIGI HADID

Find your zen

Even the most badass of babes needs a moment of luxurious laziness at the end of a longggg cvnty day. Kick off those heels, run that bubble bath and re-energize – you can pause the drama whenever you like! Tomorrow is another day to slay, but right now it's time to do *absolutely nothing*.

I'm strong,
and I'm powerful,
and I'm beautiful
at the same time.

SERENA WILLIAMS

*Stay afraid,
but do it anyway.
What's important
is the action.*

CARRIE FISHER

I'm hot AF

I love to see a young girl go out and grab the world by the lapels.

MAYA ANGELOU

You only live once, but if you do it right, once is enough.

MAE WEST

Ciao, babe!

Babe, it's been fun. We've walked, we've talked and we've dished up legendary levels of diva. You now have all the tools to turn heads and to thrive in the spotlight and *slay it your way*. So, all there is left to do is go forth and *serve cvnt*.

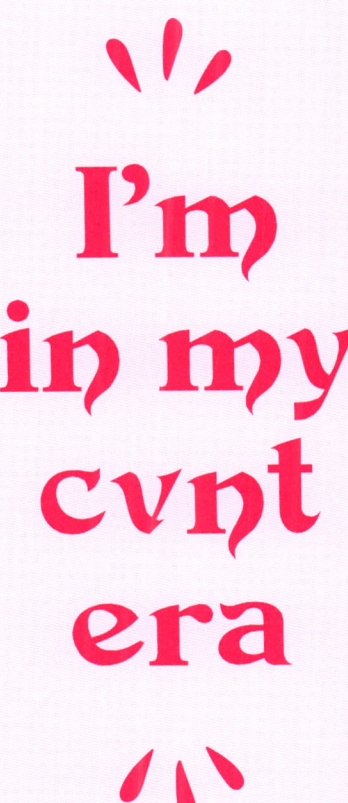

Have you enjoyed this book?
If so, find us on Facebook
at Summersdale Publishers,
on Twitter/X at @Summersdale
and on Instagram, TikTok and
Bluesky at @summersdalebooks
and get in touch.

We'd love to hear from you!

www.summersdale.com

Image Credits

p.4 & p.160 – lips © Luis Line/Shutterstock.com